TRUSTING HIS PROCESS

THE POWER OF LOVING YOURSELF THE WAY GOD LOVES YOU

CANDICE A. WINGATE

EDITED BY

NICOLE QUEEN

VISION PUBLISHING
HOUSE

Vision Publishing House
support@vision-publishinghouse.com
www.vision-publishinghouse.com

ISBN: 978-1-955297-71-4 (print)

This book is established to provide information and inspiration to all readers. It is designed with the understanding that the author is not engaged to render any psychological, legal, or any other kind of professional advice. The content is the sole expression of the author. The author is not liable for any physical, psychological, emotional, financial, or commercial damages, including, but not limited to special, incidental, consequential, or other damages. All readers are responsible for their own choices, actions, and results.

He hath made every thing beautiful in his time. Also he hath set the world in their heart, so that no man can find out the work that God maketh from the beginning to the end

— Ecclesiastes 3:11

Contents

Opening Prayer

Dear God,

You are the lover of my soul! I am thankful that You took Your time to make me a masterpiece (Ephesians 2:10). I am fearfully and wonderfully made; marvelous are Your works, and my soul knows that very well (Psalms 139:14). Lord, help me to see myself the way You see me. Help me discover my real, authentic self and appreciate every fiber of who I am and exactly who You have called me to be. Help me to be a vessel through which the very essence of love flows, that I may be an example of humility, peace, patience, self-control, joy, and love in Your Kingdom.

As I continue to walk diligently in bold and courageous faith for the call that is on my life, pour out Your favor on me like the land flowing with milk and honey, always in abundant fertility. Thank You for the abundant fertility of all the fruit in me, waiting to bear and never wither because You are the vine, and I am the branch (John 15:5). Cut off everything that is not like You, Jehovah. I bind up everything in my life that opposes Your goodness in me. I surrender myself and my life to Your divine will and purpose. Your plans are to prosper me and not to harm me (Jeremiah 29:11), so I put my faith and trust in You, God.

Show me how I can better love myself and who You've created me to be, so I can love those around me in the same way.

Lord, I pray to be the best Kingdom version of myself. I thank You that Your love is kind, patient, does not brag or boast, and is not self-seeking (1 Corinthians 13:4). God, You are love (1 John 4:7), and You are the greatest example of love, as You laid down the life of Your only begotten Son for my salvation and redemption (John 3:16).

You did not give me a spirit of fear, but of power, love, and a sound mind (2 Timothy 1:7). So even when trials and tribulations hit, I shall fear no evil. I will walk in bold faith, believing I am purposeful and created with the intent to walk on water like Peter and to storm through fires like Daniel in the den. It gives me great joy to allow Your love to work in me and through me in various ways. May Your love forever be what anchors me in my healing and forever binds my soul to You.

In Jesus' Name, I pray.
Amen.

AUTHOR'S NOTE

> *"But God, being [so very] rich in mercy, because of His great and wonderful love with which He loved us, even when we were [spiritually] dead and separated from Him because of our sins, He made us [spiritually] alive together with Christ (for by His grace – His undeserved favor and mercy – you have been saved from God's judgement)."*

— EPHESIANS 2:4-5 (AMP)

Dear readers,

In my darkest moments and 12-year battle with depression, postpartum, anxiety attacks, suicide attempts, and loss of self-esteem, I tried hard to love myself and figure out who I was. I was fighting for a reason to live, and I couldn't find one, even when I had a husband and three babies who I needed to love and who loved me. But the truth is, it's hard to truly love others when you are struggling to love yourself. Literally, you don't know yourself, and even worse, you don't know how to love yourself. After my fifth suicide attempt, I finally realized that God wasn't giving up on me, so I didn't want to give up on myself. Thankfully, He placed an amazing woman of God and prophetess in my life who helped me take the time to build a relationship with God— learning about Him and the way He viewed me. I began to find an overwhelming amount of peace, joy, and love in my life—not just for myself but for those around me, as well. I was finally able to pour back into my family the love they needed and deserved.

My personal faith walk is the inspiration for this devotional. I'd like to dedicate it first back to God for inspiring me to write this for my daughter, who will one day go through her own tribulations, and to all the women who struggle mentally, emotionally, physically, and spiritually the way I did. A continuing cycle of torment from the enemy keeps you in a stagnated place of fear and lack of self-love so that you never find the strength to move forward in your destiny and identity in God. But today, I urge you to say, "Not today, devil, get your filthy hands off me! You don't own me, and I will no longer fall victim to your lies!" It is time for you to start viewing yourself the way God views you so you can see the beauty and value in who you are and the way God created you— not the way society or the church views you.

First, you need to know and understand who God is and what He has done for you to truly appreciate Him and yourself. You must form an intimate relationship with God to experience His love in a way you couldn't without Him. Experiencing His love allows us to appreciate the life He has given us when we focus less on materialistic things and viewpoints, while starting to value the Holy Spirit, whom God has given us so we can be more like Him. God is raising the standard, and many of us have been too comfortable faking the funk! Although looking and feeling beautiful isn't a bad thing, it's not your perfectly glammed outside appearance that God focuses on. He wants to use you to break generational curses and kick down the doors of the enemy's facades.

He's empowering and using the women who are broken, but completely sold out for Him! Those are the women who are willing to be used, willing to obey, willing to heal, and willing to *love*! We need to understand that we may not be perfect; we are a work in progress, but that doesn't make us any less beautiful or less fearfully and wonderfully made. Even with the quirks, say this with me: "*I am intentionally made, and I am intentionally loved.*" I was put here on purpose and for a purpose, and everything that happens to me—good or bad—God is still working it out for my good.

My prayer is that this devotional helps you go beyond your outward appearance and the simplistic ways society has told you what love is. I pray that you will dive in deeper and go through the real process of change so that God's love comes naturally to you. I pray that you'll be willing to share that love—and hopefully, this devotional—with another woman in need. The title and chapters of this devotional were part of my personal process, and the messages talk about what that process looks like. I believe it is and will be the process for many of you. Take your time to meditate, allowing God to pour His love into your heart, as you self-examine and allow the Holy Spirit to speak to you.

With Love,
Candice A. Wingate

Day One
Know Who You Belong To

One of the most humanistic ways of feeling loved is knowing that someone claims you and cares for you in an indescribable way—someone who genuinely wants the best for you. The most authentic example of this kind of love is like that between a parent and child because it's the only relationship where you don't have to do anything or fully know the person to love them.

The moment I gave birth to my firstborn, and the doctors handed me my baby boy, I took one long look into his eyes, and this indescribable feeling came rushing over me. I wanted to cry. I didn't know how I was going to be able to care for this newborn or if I would even be good at it. All I knew was that I loved him with my whole heart and soul, and I was willing to do anything to protect him. I felt that way with all three of my children. It's a feeling that truly can't be explained.

I'd like to believe that God feels the same way about us. Romans 8:14 teaches that those who allow themselves to be led by His Spirit are called His children, and He is their Father.

Because God is our Father and the epitome of love, when we allow His Spirit to lead us, we can literally feel His love all around us, especially in His grace.

God loves us so much that He sacrificed His only Son by bringing

Him into our world, only for Him to die on a cross for sins we couldn't redeem on our own. This sacrifice allows us to live through Christ and have the option of eternal life with God (John 3:16). That's an indescribable feeling. Think about the fact that Christ was beaten, whipped, bruised, and crowned with thorns (Mark 15:17)—and so much more—just so He could have a relationship with you, personally! Let's pause for a moment and consider the lengths you would be willing to go to have a relationship with Him.

We all know a parent who would literally sacrifice a limb to save their child. You may be that parent. It may sound humorous, but there are countless stories of mothers and fathers who have lied for their children, bailed them out of jail with their only savings, put themselves in danger, prioritized their child's feelings over their spouse's, and more. The list goes on. However, even though they are your children, and you know you'd do anything for them. Eventually, enough becomes enough. It's hard to keep protecting them in that manner when you're neglecting yourself and everyone else around you; at the end of the day, you're only human.

What makes God's sacrificial love for His children so powerful is that His love is so great it can never be repaid, yet we get to reap the biggest blessing: He walks with us and talks to us, with His Spirit guiding us through this journey called life. God sacrificed His one and only Son for generations upon generations of people. We, on the other hand, can only sacrifice for ourselves because we can't bear to see what we birthed come to ruin.

Children grow up, and at a certain age, they leave their parents. As God's children, this is the only parent-child relationship where it's not frowned upon to remain with your Father for the rest of your life. Age is not a factor to God. The older we get, the more that love increases, if we draw close to Him. The more intimate we become, building a strong relationship with Him, the more we can maturely reflect and recognize His hand over our lives. As we reflect, we become more aware of how much He cares for us, in all the ways He's protected us, even when we thought no one was there. God knows how hard and challenging life can be.

As His children, when we stay connected to God and allow

ourselves to be led by His Spirit, we are no longer slaves (Galatians 4:7) to the things that block us from being loved and receiving love from God. We receive 24/7 protection, love, and care that only a fathering God can give. You are a child of God, and knowing that should bring you great comfort, as His top priority is ensuring you know you are loved and cared for.

* * *

DAY #1 PRAYER

Gracious and loving Father,

Thank You for choosing me to be one of Your own. I thank You that there is no mountain too high or valley too low to keep You away from me. Thank You for sacrificing Your one true Son on a cross for me, so that I will never perish but have eternal life with You (John 3:16).

Thank You, Father, that as my Shepherd, You let me lie down in green pastures and lead me beside still waters. You refresh and restore my soul and guide me in the paths of righteousness (Psalm 23:2-3). Thank You that Your Word says You go before me and with me, and You will never leave me nor forsake me (Deuteronomy 31:8).

Thank You, God, that I can walk confidently on this earth knowing who I truly belong to! I am Your heir, and You are an amazing Father!

In Jesus' Name, I pray.
Amen.

IMPORTANT SCRIPTURES

(Amplified Version)

> For all who are allowing themselves to be led by the Spirit of God are sons of God.

— ROMANS 8:14

> For God so loved and dearly prized the world, that He gave His only begotten Son, so that whoever believes and trusts in Him shall not perish but have eternal life.

— JOHN 3:16

> They dressed Him up in purple, and after twisting a crown of thorns, they placed it on Him.

— MARK 15:17

> Therefore, you are no longer a slave, but a son; and if a son, then also an heir through God.

— GALATIANS 4:7

CAPTURE YOUR THOUGHTS

Utilize this space below to record what comes to your mind.

_____

_____

_____

_____

_____

_____

_____

_____

_____

_____

_____

_____

_____

_____

_____

_____

_____

_____

_____

_____

_____

_____

_____

_____

_____

_____

_____

_____

_____

PERSONAL REFLECTION

1. Share your highlights from *Day One: "Know Who You Belong To."*

_____

_____

_____

_____

_____

_____

2. God sacrificed His one and only Son to have a relationship with you. What are you willing to sacrifice to have a relationship with God?

_____

_____

_____

_____

_____

_____

3. What confidence can you gain from being a Child of God?

_____

_____

_____

_____

_____

_____

4. What did you learn about God today?

_____

_____

_____

_____

_____

_____

5. What did you learn about yourself today?

_____

_____

_____

_____

_____

_____

The way God
made me is
Good!

DAY TWO
I MAY NOT BE PERFECT, BUT I'M GOOD

Naturally, because we are born into sin, the last thing we might consider ourselves is "good." Every day, when I wake up and when I lay my head down to sleep, there is always something I know I've done that day that wasn't... "good." Maybe it was the way I yelled at my kids, the way I slacked off at work, the disheartening feeling when I forget to pray, or when I put my fleshly desires before my family —and most importantly—before God. Before I know it, I've planted a million little negative seeds in my head that take root, deeming me unworthy, unlovable, a bad mother, a bad wife, and a bad Christian. Instead of seeing myself as good, but simply imperfect, I only saw myself as "bad" and "broken" because I was failing to meet my own version of what I thought God's standards were for me. The truth is, sometimes, those seeds of negative thinking become hard to uproot.

If this is something you have struggled with or are currently struggling with, remember 1 Timothy 4:4, which states, "For everything God created is good." Find peace in knowing that because God created you, you are good.

You are good when you make mistakes. You are good when you're hurting and in emotional pain. You are good when you accidentally lash out, and you're still good when you're struggling to align with God's will for your life—even when you're unsure of what that looks like. The point is, we are not good when we are perfect, and we are not good because we are perfect—there's no such thing. We are good solely because we are created by God. We are His masterpiece (Ephesians 2:10).

When we give thanks to God in the midst of confusion, hurt, pain, and struggle, we allow the Holy Spirit to work on our hearts. The Holy Spirit guides us through our pain with the Word of God, reminding us of who we are, who we belong to, and who is really in control. The Holy Spirit encourages us through the remembrance of Scripture when we are not feeling our best. Don't block God's gift by shutting Him out and allowing the enemy to feed disbelief about yourself and God, leaving you filled with hurt and anger. Make room for the Holy Spirit to pour out God's truth about who you are so you can confidently rest in His grace and mercy.

Thanking God shows gratitude and appreciation for ourselves—for the fact that there's only one of me, and it doesn't get any better than me. That's why I'm willing to work on me! This gratitude is an understanding that, although I may be struggling with my self-esteem or character, I'm thankful the Lord is with me, and I'm not in this battle alone. Viewing ourselves the way God views us brings forth a particular love and thoughtful concern for our image and personality. It won't always be easy, but this constant appreciation will help change how we view ourselves and others. If we strive to see ourselves as good, even when we struggle in our sin, it's a constant reminder that we are good because God created us—and He created us to lean on Him! I'm so glad that our Creator never intended for us to live life alone. I'm so glad that, even as imperfect humans, God still calls us good.

* * *

DAY #2 PRAYER

Gracious and loving Father,

I am thankful that because You've created me, I am good. It is not by my works but by Your love for me that I am here. Holy Spirit, train me to capture every negative thought about me that exalts itself higher than God almighty and bring it into the obedience of Christ.

I rebuke every demonic message from the enemy that tries to lower my self-worth and self-esteem. I pray the weight of cynicism and pessimism will no longer be my portion and my outlook and perspectives are changing in the way of the Lord's. I pray to not be so critical of myself.

Help me to not create my own material standard of what good and bad is, but lean on what God views as good. Because You love me Lord, I vow to love myself. Lord, help me to extend the same grace and mercy You give to me to others. What a privilege it is to be loved and created by You, Lord.

In Jesus' name, I pray.
Amen.

IMPORTANT SCRIPTURES

(Amplified Version)

For everything God created is good.

— 1 TIMOTHY 4:4-5

For we are His workmanship, created in Christ Jesus for good works, which God prepared beforehand, so that we would walk in them.

— EPHESIANS 2:10

We demolish arguments and every pretension that sets itself up against the knowledge of God, and we take captive every thought to make it obedient to Christ.

2 CORINTHIANS 10:5

CAPTURE YOUR THOUGHTS

Utilize this space below to record what comes to your mind.

_____

_____

_____

_____

_____

_____

_____

_____

_____

_____

_____

_____

_____

_____

_____

_____

_____

_____

_____

_____

_____

_____

_____

_____

_____

_____

_____

_____

_____

_____

_____

_____

_____

PERSONAL REFLECTION

1. Share your highlights from *Day Two: "I May Not Be Perfect, But I'm Good."*

_____

_____

_____

_____

_____

_____

2. What negative "seeds" have you been planting in your mind about yourself? How do you plan to uproot them?

_____

_____

_____

_____

_____

_____

_____

3. How can you show gratitude to God even when you're hurting?

_____

_____

_____

_____

_____

_____

_____

4. What did you learn about God today?

_____

_____

_____

_____

_____

_____

5. What did you learn about yourself today?

_____

_____

_____

_____

_____

_____

My life is
Purposeful!

Day Three

Understanding Your Purpose

I t's always been hard to love the things we're unsure of, and living a life full of unknowns can make you question every decision you make. To be honest, that's where most of my depression stemmed from when I was younger—being unsure of who I was and what I should be doing with my life. It can be frustrating when you're carrying a laundry basket full of responsibilities, and you don't know why you must accomplish them, or if they will bring you any type of success or satisfaction. However, we can find fulfillment in God and His purpose for our lives.

I have learned that I am not here on this earth simply because I want to be, but because God chose me to be here. God's Word says in Jeremiah 1:5, "Before I formed you in the womb, I knew you, and before you were born, I consecrated you."

Jehovah thought of you and loved you before you were even created. The very fact that He wanted you here on this earth shows that He was intentional about how He created you and intentional about the purpose for which you were created.

Many times, we question what that purpose is, and then we try to "do" and focus so much on trying to accomplish certain accolades the world says will add value to our lives, thus deeming us more successful.

We've been taught that the more "successful" we are, the more purpose we live in.

The world says: get that doctorate degree, buy that home with the white picket fence, have at least two kids, and be an entrepreneur. And if no one on Facebook sees the three vacations you took around the world, then apparently, you're not living your best life.

Praise God! He doesn't think the way the world does. God values us for who we are and who He created us to be, not for what we accomplish in our daily jobs. While being educated and driven to pursue your dreams is not a bad thing, take note that in God's eyes, a doctorate degree doesn't make you any better than someone with a GED; being a homeowner doesn't make you any better than someone who rents an apartment or lives on the street.

What's most important is drawing close to God (James 4:8), striving to live in a manner pleasing to Him, and seeking to bring Him glory. We were created to have a relationship with Him, so the most purposeful thing we can do is just that.

Ultimately, there will be a decision and a sacrifice we must make if we wish to have a relationship with God. We must abandon the way we were taught to view ourselves and our purpose, so that we can live in the manner God calls us to.

The relationship is how God calls us out and sets us apart (Psalm 4:3). It allows God to speak to us, guiding our every step and making us the best version of ourselves—the most productive for His Kingdom (Psalm 37:23). God's plans are to prosper us and not to harm us (Jeremiah 29:11), so who better to give us the purpose we've all been seeking?

That purpose and feeling of fulfillment will lead you to appreciate and love yourself more, knowing that you have something important to offer the world. God, Himself, commissioned you by creating you with purpose and sending you forth to connect with others He has done the same for.

Please know that you are valuable in God's eyes! Your relationship with Him above all else is your purpose. "Seek the Kingdom and His righteousness [His way of doing and being right—the attitude and character of God], and all these things will be given to you also" (Matthew

6:33). Start seeing yourself as one of His best masterpieces (Ephesians 2:10), and know that every part of you and everything that happens to you has a purpose.

* * *

DAY #3 PRAYER

Gracious and loving Father,

I am beautifully and fearfully made, handcrafted with destiny and purpose. Even on the days I cannot find the strength to love myself and on days I see no purpose, You still love me unconditionally. God, You are faithful and make no mistakes. I thank You for my life—the life into which You breathed Your breath. I am part of a royal priesthood because You are my Father. El Roi, You are the God who sees me.

I pray against all wicked spirits that try to keep me in a place of stagnation, so that I don't move forward on the paths You have set before me. I pray to hear a Word from You that will speak to my purpose and touch the souls of those connected to me. Your Word says to draw close to You, and You will draw close to me. I pray that the fulfillment of building a relationship with You will lead me to understand my purpose and value myself as one of Your masterful creations. Thank You for Your ever-abounding grace.

In Jesus' precious name, I pray.
Amen.

Important Scriptures

(Amplified Version)

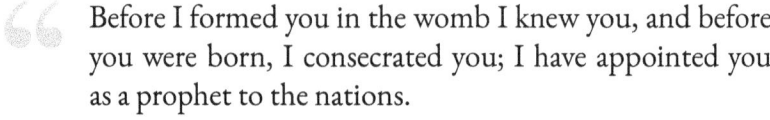

> Before I formed you in the womb I knew you, and before you were born, I consecrated you; I have appointed you as a prophet to the nations.
>
> — Jeremiah 1:5

> But know that the LORD has set apart for Himself the godly man. The LORD hears and responds when I call to Him.
>
> — Psalm 4:3

> Come close to God and He will come close to you.
>
> — James 4:8

> The steps of a [good and righteous] man are directed and established by the Lord, and he delights in his way [and blesses his path].
>
> — Psalm 37:23

> For I know the plans and thoughts that I have for you, says the Lord, plans for peace and well-being and not for disaster, to give you a future and a hope.
>
> — Jeremiah 29:11

> For we are His workmanship, created in Christ Jesus for good works, which God prepared beforehand, so that we would walk in them.
>
> — Ephesians 2:10

Seek the Kingdom and His righteousness [His way of doing and being right – the attitude and character of God], and all these things will be given to you also.

— MATTHEW 6:33

CAPTURE YOUR THOUGHTS

Utilize this space below to record what comes to your mind.

_____
_____
_____
_____
_____
_____
_____
_____
_____
_____
_____
_____
_____
_____
_____
_____
_____
_____
_____
_____
_____
_____
_____
_____
_____
_____
_____
_____
_____
_____
_____

PERSONAL REFLECTION

1. Share your highlights from *Day Three: "Understanding Your Purpose."*

_____
_____
_____
_____
_____
_____

2. How does God's view of purpose combat your current thoughts on living a purposeful life?

_____
_____
_____
_____
_____
_____

3. How will you start strengthening your relationship with God so that you can hear him more clearly regarding your purpose and destiny?

_____
_____
_____
_____
_____
_____

4. What did you learn about God today?

_____

_____

_____

_____

_____

_____

5. What did you learn about yourself today?

_____

_____

_____

_____

_____

_____

I am clothed in

Strength &

Dignity!

Day Four

Metamorphosis

etamorphosis is the process of transformation. It's a change in the form or nature of a thing or person into a completely different one, by natural or supernatural means.

As someone who purged my closet multiple times a year, I always battled with what I needed to keep and what I wanted to hold on to, even though I knew I had outgrown those things. They were no longer part of my style or the way I wanted to clothe myself. Looking back, I now know it's because, at that time, I dressed myself based on a societal identity, not one that was firmly rooted in God.

From high school to college, my style and choice of clothing changed drastically. I went from being dressed by my mom to finally being an "adult" with the freedom to dress myself. In reality, that meant being covered up throughout high school to being half-naked in college, in an effort to look appealing to the opposite sex.

However, the tides changed in my early twenties as a newborn Christian. At that time, I became a wife and mother, and my style quickly changed to accommodate the comforts of raising children, cooking, cleaning, working, and serving in ministry.

I swiftly realized the many "hats" I had to wear as a woman who was married, had kids, worked, and grew in God. I also realized that not all of those "hats" and "clothes" suited the kind of woman God was calling me to be and love.

During my time of evolving, I battled with postpartum depression and clothed myself in self-hate, anxiety, rejection, as well as mental and physical abuse. I overdosed on pills and allowed the enemy to whisper negative thoughts and visions in my mind, leaving me feeling disgusted and defeated. Every day, I dressed myself in those emotions and feelings, and every day it became harder to operate as a nurturing mom, loving wife, and caring neighbor. Those clothes of self-hate, anxiety, and depression are not versatile, and they can only be worn one way.

The Lord began to show me three things I could have total control over: my attitude, character, and effort. One day, it finally clicked—I no longer wanted to dress myself in clothes that didn't suit the beautiful woman of God I knew I was born to be. If I wanted control over my mind and feelings, I had to undress myself from those emotions and feelings that had ruled me for so long and redress myself in God's armor (Ephesians 6:13-17), His Word, and His Spirit, which He blessed me with.

If you're reading this and can relate, I believe God is using my example to say to you, metaphorically: throw out the clothes in your closet that you no longer desire to wear. It's not your identity. It's not what makes you, you. Don't hold on to things for keepsakes. I'm creating a new identity of Christ in you, but the more your closet is packed with things of your old nature, the harder it will be to find room for the gems I have given you to change into. I have prepared and adorned a new wardrobe for you to wear—one that will give you strength and courage! Abide in Me as I in you, and see the fruits of your labor prosper!

 Strength and dignity are her clothing, and her position is strong and secure; and she smiles at the future [knowing that she and her family are prepared].

— PROVERBS 31:25 (AMP)

The more I stripped myself of my old ways of thinking by paying attention to my thoughts and casting down everything that opposed God's goodness in me, the more I slowly started morphing into a warrior! I never quit or cowered to the enemy. I changed from suffering and shame to strength and dignity. Now, I smile knowing my future is bright because I believe in God, stand on His Word, and my family is safe from the person I used to be. How many of you are ready and willing to strip off the clothes of depression, anxiety, and self-hate and morph into the fearless warrior God has destined you to be? The battles may feel back-to-back, but God is with you! And you only grow stronger mentally, emotionally, and spiritually when you don't give up!

When you begin to change your clothes and strip yourself from the bondage of how the enemy desires you to view yourself, the more God will reveal Himself to you and show you who you are and to whom you belong. When He does that, believe Him! Those beliefs of the truth will allow love to penetrate your heart and change how you view your true self. How does one know their true self? Your true self is the image of God—His holiness, His righteousness. By casting away what serves the part of you that wants to sulk in your own grief of living, you will start to feel lighter and finally be able to produce His fruit of joy, peace, love, humility, and self-control. That is your true self because it's the part of Christ that lives in you.

* * *

DAY #4 PRAYER

Gracious and loving Father,

Thank You for loving me. Thank You for showing me a way out of my own grief and sorrow. Thank You for changing my clothes from rags to riches. You are my light and my salvation. The love You have for me is continually teaching me to have that same love for myself. I pray to be properly suited in the armor You have given me whenever the enemy tries to attack. I am confident because You did not give me the spirit of fear, but the power of love and a sound mind! I declare and decree that I have a sound mind to rebuke every lie the enemy has ever spoken over my life because I know Your Word, and it is my firm foundation. I give You the glory, honor, and praise for the changes You have made and will continue to make in me and through me. Transform and renew me, Lord— for I am Yours.

In Jesus' mighty name, I pray.
Amen.

IMPORTANT SCRIPTURES

(Amplified Version)

66 Therefore, if anyone is in Christ, he is a new creature; the old things have passed away. Behold, new things have come.

— 2 CORINTHIANS 5:17

66 And do not be conformed to this world, but be transformed by the renewing of your mind, so that you may prove what the will of God is, that which is good and acceptable and perfect.

— ROMANS 12:2

66 Strength and dignity are her clothing, and her position is strong and secure; And she smiles at her future.

— PROVERBS 31:25

66 May the God of hope fill you with all joy and peace in believing that by the power of the Holy Spirit you will abound in hope and overflow with confidence in His promise.

— ROMANS 15:13

66 Therefore, put on the complete armor of God, so that you will be able to resist and stand your ground in the evil day, and having done everything, to stand firm. So, stand firm and hold your ground, having tighten the wide band of truth around your waist and having put on the breastplate of righteousness, and having strapped on your feet

the gospel of peace in preparation, above all, lift up the shield of faith with which you can extinguish all the flaming arrows of the evil one. And take the helmet of salvation, and the sword of the spirit, which is the Word of God.

— EPHESIANS 6:13-17

CAPTURE YOUR THOUGHTS

Utilize this space below to record what comes to your mind.

PERSONAL REFLECTION

1. Share your highlights from *Day Four: "Metamorphosis."*

_____

_____

_____

_____

_____

_____

2. What types of "clothes" do you need to change out of? How will you begin to clothe yourself differently?

_____

_____

_____

_____

_____

3. What pieces of the Armor of God are you missing? How can you begin to wear them confidently?

_____

_____

_____

_____

_____

4. What did you learn about God today?

_____

_____

_____

_____

_____

_____

5. What did you learn about yourself today?

_____

_____

_____

_____

_____

_____

I am
Healed!

DAY FIVE

NOT EASILY BROKEN

The world's idea of loving oneself often stems from pampering the body with materialistic gifts and undergoing makeovers. For example, when you're sad or upset, the common response is to buy food or something to make you feel better, or to change your outward appearance—like chopping off your hair—as if these actions will somehow make you a better version of yourself, one that someone else might appreciate more. However, no matter how many times we modify our bodies, our heart condition remains the same because outward changes don't remove the deep hurt and pain inside. It's only masked until someone else comes along and rips the bandage off, stabbing you in the same painful spot all over again. If we never get to the root of the problem, every time something traumatic happens in our lives, it can chip away at our thoughts and self-worth, leaving us broken and vulnerable to the enemy and his schemes.

Thankfully, we can be vulnerable with God and trust Him with those broken pieces, because every part of our mind and body was uniquely created by Him according to the plan and purpose He has for our lives. He already knows the things we struggle with, and He sees and acknowledges all the ways we've been hurting.

In this "60 seconds or less" era, it's important to know that God takes His time with us. We don't have to rush the process. With objects, things can easily be glued or sewn back together to "look" whole again, but most of the time, you can still see the cracks. With God, however, He doesn't just glue what was broken—He heals and binds (Psalm 147:3)!

When we humbly go before God with the pain in our lives, He reveals the problem and shows us how to fix it. If we don't take affirmative action by being extremely vulnerable before God with our hurt and pain, we deny Him access to mend, heal, and restore us (1 Peter 5:6-7). But when we approach God with open arms, He pours out His Spirit of peace, love, and joy to refresh us. He allows us to hope again, and He counsels us through our journey of healing (Romans 5:5, Isaiah 44:3). If we give Him the opportunity, He will use people, places, and most importantly His Word to impart His view of overcoming and teach us how to renew our minds and forgive ourselves and others for the pain we've endured.

When God heals you, the parts of you that were broken—mentally, physically, spiritually, and emotionally—are no longer visible. People can no longer see the "cracks" that once allowed them to come in and reopen your wounds, breaking pieces of you that you need to love.

When God heals, we are made whole in Him. What used to hurt us and cause us pain now bounces off this beautiful, shiny, strong new vessel that God Himself has molded together (Isaiah 64:8).

* * *

DAY #5 PRAYER

Gracious and loving Father,

I come humbly before Your mighty hand and cast all my cares and anxieties at Your feet. I'm grateful that You are the God who heals the brokenhearted and binds up their wounds. I submit to You that I cannot work this out on my own, and I need You to carry me through this pain. I cast my worries into a sea of forgetfulness and trust that You will order and direct my steps, establishing me in all Your ways.

Although the weapons may form, they shall not prosper! I decree that healing is my portion in the name of Jesus! I plead the Blood over my life and my mind! Lord, You are the Potter, and I am the clay. Mold me. Renew me. Change me. I am fully Yours.

In Jesus' precious and mighty Name, I pray.
Amen.

IMPORTANT SCRIPTURES

(Amplified Version)

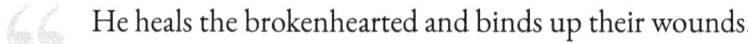

> He heals the brokenhearted and binds up their wounds.

— PSALM 147:3

> Therefore, humble yourselves under the mighty hand of God, so that He may exalt you at the appropriate time, casting all your cares on Him, for He cares about you.

— 1 PETER 5:6-7

> Such hope never disappoints us, because God's love has been abundantly poured out within our hearts through the Holy Spirit who was given to us.

— ROMANS 5:5

> For I will pour out water on him who is thirsty, and streams on the dry ground; I will pour out My spirit on your offspring and My blessing on your descendants.

— ISAIAH 44:3

> Yet, O Lord, you are our Father; we are the clay, and you are our potter, and we all are the work of your hand.

— ISAIAH 64:8

CAPTURE YOUR THOUGHTS

Utilize this space below to record what comes to your mind.

_____

_____

_____

_____

_____

_____

_____

_____

_____

_____

_____

_____

_____

_____

_____

_____

_____

_____

_____

_____

_____

_____

_____

_____

_____

_____

_____

_____

_____

_____

PERSONAL REFLECTION

1. Share your highlights from *Day Five: "Not Easily Broken."*

_____
_____
_____
_____
_____
_____

2. What are some things you need healing from today?

_____
_____
_____
_____
_____
_____

3. How can you continue to love yourself and trust God through your process of healing?

_____
_____
_____
_____
_____
_____

4. What did you learn about God today?

_____

_____

_____

_____

_____

_____

5. What did you learn about yourself today?

_____

_____

_____

_____

_____

_____

I'm more than a
Conqueror!

Day Six

It Takes Courage

A *conqueror* is a person who conquers a place or people, to carry off the victory and come out victorious. He or she is also one who attains mastery over sense consciousness.

To be courageous, you have boldness and confidence. It's the quality of being ready and willing to face negative situations, potentially involving danger or pain.

In Biblical times, when an army conquered a people or place, it meant they were victorious in the battle or war they fought. They now ruled over that people and place, and they carried the spoils of their victory. This meant they had access to the valuable possessions the enemy once owned. These were moments of great rejoicing!

In the first chapter of Joshua, God tells Joshua to take his place and lead the remaining Israelites into the land of Canaan, "the land flowing with milk and honey." However, when they arrive, they realize it is already occupied by a group of people, and they must conquer it to access what God has promised them. In this context, God urges Joshua to be strong and courageous three times.

The first time, God says it as He commissions Joshua to lead the Israelites into the land promised to their ancestors. Then, God emphasizes it again by telling Joshua to be careful to follow His commands in accordance with the entire law given to Moses, and not to turn to the left or right, so that he may be prosperous in his journey. Finally, God commands Joshua to be bold and courageous once more, assuring him that He will be with him wherever he goes.

Let's first acknowledge that God chose Joshua and gave him a specific mission. After giving Joshua this mission, He provided specific instructions to ensure his journey would be prosperous. After the mission and instructions, God validated both Joshua and the mission by promising to be with him wherever he went.

Let's break down the three ways being bold and courageous relates to loving yourself and where that confidence comes from.

First, on Day 3, we talked about how our lives are purposeful. Because God knew us before we were in our mother's womb, He already knew the battles we'd have to fight and the wars He has destined us to win. Joshua is an example that God specifically chooses His warriors, and that includes you! So, we ought to be bold and courageous because we were born for this mission.

The road was never meant to be easy, but it has always had purpose, destiny, and freedom tied to it. God tells Joshua to be bold and courageous and to lead the Israelites into the Promised Land because God had already promised it to him and his people—they just had to trust in God and take it! I believe right now God is telling you that peace, love, joy, healing, and freedom are already your portion. You may currently be in a state of depression, hopelessness, or loneliness. Whatever state you're in that has you feeling low and stagnated, God is saying, "Get up, be bold and courageous, because what I have in store for you is already promised to you." I know you're hurting. I know you've been wondering when you'll receive your breakthrough. The truth is, you must get up and go after it as I have commanded. You are the one I am sending, so be bold and courageous because I've already prepared and commissioned you for this assignment. You must learn to fight for what God has already promised you and be confident that because He promised it, you will receive it.

Second, after God gave Joshua a specific mission, He gave him specific instructions. These instructions were to do everything in accordance with the law that His servant Moses commanded. This teaches us that being bold and courageous also means that our journey will be prosperous by following God's Word, even when others around us won't.

As you go through your process of healing and accepting love, don't make hurt and pain your idols. Be bold and courageous by pushing forward and staying in God's Word so you can remain connected to Him and the Holy Spirit. Follow His every instruction and let your relationship with Him keep you from straying onto a path He didn't call you to take. This will ensure that your relationship with God and your journey of learning to love yourself will be successful.

Third, finally, being bold and courageous means stepping out and doing what God has commanded because you know and have faith that He is with you! God validated Joshua's mission by reminding him that He commanded him to be bold and courageous because He would be with him wherever he went. God made it clear that He was supporting Joshua's obedience to Him.

Whatever your journey requires, don't be intimidated by the hurdles that may try to block you from receiving God's love and His promises. The enemy will try to keep you from believing in God, but obedience to God will lead you to victory; it will come swiftly because God will guide and support your every step!

Can you see it now? Everything you need to be more than a conqueror is already in you! Will you allow the enemy to take control of your mind, thoughts, and emotions? Or, will you kick down the door the enemy keeps knocking on with the power and authority God has given you to conquer your mind, body, and thoughts— proclaiming life and healing over them? There is a Promised Land of peace, love, and joy waiting for you to embrace. So, what are you waiting for? Be bold and courageous, today!

* * *

DAY #6 PRAYER

Gracious and loving Father,

Thank You, that even when it looks like I'm surrounded, I'm truly surrounded by You. Thank You for going before me, behind me, and all around me. Your Word says that You will never leave me nor forsake me. Thank You for giving me the authority to conquer everything that is not of You and not like You. Just as You commanded Joshua to be bold and courageous, I will be bold and courageous against my enemies and the demonic principalities of this world, knowing that You will be with me wherever I go. As I go into battle each day, I will suit up with the full armor of God, knowing that You won't fail—and You've never failed me yet. Thank You for being my fortress and strong tower, my present help in times of trouble. When I feel like I can't go on, I can always look to the hills from where my help comes. I am more than a conqueror because, Lord, You strengthen me. I will not be dismayed, and I will not cower down. I will boldly move forward toward the promises You have made me. I will rejoice, knowing that every day, I am one step closer to claiming what is already mine!

In Jesus' Name, I pray.
Amen.

IMPORTANT SCRIPTURES

(Amplified Version)

Yet in all these things we are more than conquerors and gain an overwhelming victory through Him who loved us.

— ROMANS 8:37

Be strong and confident and courageous, for you will give this people as an inheritance the land which I swore to their fathers to give them. Only be strong and very courageous; be careful to do in accordance with the entire law which Moses My servant commanded you; do not turn from it to the right or to the left, so that you may prosper and be successful wherever you go. This Book of the Law shall not depart from your mouth, but you shall read it day and night, so that you may be careful to do in accordance with all that is written in it; for then you will make your way prosperous, and then you will be successful. Have I not commanded you? Be strong and courageous! Do not be terrified or dismayed (intimidated), for the Lord your God is with you wherever you go.

— JOSHUA 1:6-9

CAPTURE YOUR THOUGHTS

Utilize this space below to record what comes to your mind.

_____
_____
_____
_____
_____
_____
_____
_____
_____
_____
_____
_____
_____
_____
_____
_____
_____
_____
_____
_____
_____
_____
_____
_____
_____
_____
_____
_____
_____
_____
_____
_____

PERSONAL REFLECTION

1. Share your highlights from *Day Six: "It Takes Courage."*

_____

_____

_____

_____

_____

_____

2. In what way is God calling you to be bold and courageous?

_____

_____

_____

_____

_____

_____

3. What personal instructions has God given you to obey?

_____

_____

_____

_____

_____

_____

4. What did you learn about God today?

_____

_____

_____

_____

_____

_____

5. What did you learn about yourself today?

_____

_____

_____

_____

_____

_____

DAY SEVEN
SEEK THE LORD AND HIS STRENGTH

In Genesis, after God spent six days thinking, dwelling, and creating the earth, He rested on the seventh day and sanctified it— making it holy and set apart from the other days. God's rest was not a rest of weariness, but a rest of being pleased, knowing the goodness and manifestation of His glory, and appreciating the wonderful works He had created.

I submit to you, as you're reading this, that the process of loving yourself and God is hard because you have not rested. You have not rested in God's peace, joy, love... His Spirit. This is not an optional task; it's a necessary and mandatory one. Life has a way of shifting you from one adventure to the next. When we don't take moments to allow the Holy Spirit to sit in us, talk to us, and rest in us, we eventually feel burdened by our daily tasks and obligations. This makes it hard to receive and release love because the workload of taking care of ourselves and our families never feels completely "finished."

We need to rest in God by spending time in His presence, praying, and reflecting on His Word to feel the fullness of His love.

One way you can do that is by consecrating a portion of your day to just focus on God, making a particular part of your day intentional and holy. 1 Chronicles 16:11 says, "Seek the Lord and His strength; seek His face continually." This is a command. God looks for those who seek Him, and He pours into them. But how can He strengthen and pour into someone who never takes the time to talk to Him? An important step in learning love is being in a relationship with God. If you don't take the time to know God, you will never build that relationship and will never be able to practice receiving and giving true love the way God intends.

A great example of this is in Luke 7:36-39, where a woman in the city, who was known as a sinner, took the time to weep and cry at Jesus' feet. She wiped her tears with the hair on her head while kissing His feet and anointing Him with the expensive alabaster vial of perfume she had brought with her. Notice that she did not let what she was known for (a sinner) stop her from seeking the Lord and being at His feet. She submitted to Jesus, showing such reverence and affection by being vulnerable with her tears and using the very hair on her head to clean His feet. Because of that, in verse 47, Jesus stands up for her in front of the Pharisees and says her sins are forgiven! What great love He pours back into those who sit at His feet.

Apart from dedicating a specific time of your day to sit with God, you must also be walking with and worshiping God in spirit and truth, as you live your life daily. When you practice physically consecrating time to focus on God, it will be easier to have a lifestyle of worship—walking and talking with Him during the busyness of your day, and allowing the Holy Spirit to guide you into God's will for your life. Talking to God throughout the day allows Him to fill and lead you, and you must trust that He will. When life starts to get out of control, or someone speaks to you in a manner that is not befitting, because you've been thinking on and dwelling with God, His Spirit will be resting on and in you. No one will be able to easily take away your peace, and there will be no stumbling blocks you won't be able to overcome.

Just as God was pleased on the seventh day with all the glorious work He had created, you can be well pleased with the work God is doing daily through you and in your life, as you sit with Him. You can rest in Him, and then repeat it all again the next day.

* * *

DAY #7 PRAYER

Gracious and loving Father,

Thank You for Your Holy Spirit. By resting in You, I find peace, joy, and love. Thank You for showing me what it means to love myself and what it means to love You. Lord, I pray for the desire to seek Your face and seek it earnestly because I know my soul depends on it. I pray to draw close to You, so You can draw close to me. Lord, help me to schedule my days, so I can spend amplified time with You. Help me to be more willing to surrender to Your will as You speak with me throughout the days. I love You, Lord. You are my strength and my strong tower; I shall forever lean on You and trust in You.

In Jesus' precious and mighty Name, I pray.
Amen.

IMPORTANT SCRIPTURES

(Amplified Version)

> Seek the Lord and His strength; Seek His face continually.

— 1 CHRONICLES 16:11

> Blessed and favored by God are those who keep His testimonies, and who seek Him and long for Him with all their heart.

— PSALM 119:2

> Come to me, all who are weary and heavily burdened, and I will give you rest.

— MATTHEW 11:28

> For the one who has once entered His rest has also rested from his labors, just as God rested from His own. Let us therefore make every effort to enter that rest, so that no one will fall by following the same example of disobedience.

— HEBREWS 4:10-11

CAPTURE YOUR THOUGHTS

Utilize this space below to record what comes to your mind.

_____

_____

_____

_____

_____

_____

_____

_____

_____

_____

_____

_____

_____

_____

_____

_____

_____

_____

_____

_____

_____

_____

_____

_____

_____

_____

_____

_____

_____

_____

_____

_____

PERSONAL REFLECTION

1. Share your highlights from *Day Seven: "Seek the Lord and His Strength."*

_____
_____
_____
_____
_____
_____

2. Is there anything preventing you from entering God's rest? How can you finally submit it to the Lord?

_____
_____
_____
_____
_____
_____

3. How will you put God first in your life?

_____
_____
_____
_____
_____

4. What did you learn about God today?

_____

_____

_____

_____

_____

_____

5. What did you learn about yourself today?

_____

_____

_____

_____

_____

_____

THE ARMOR OF GOD

As I was creating this devotional, God revealed something powerful to me. Just as He declared His work complete on the seventh day, this devotional, structured in seven days, represents my own personal journey— a three-year process of renewal and transformation. It reflects the continuous steps I had to take to strengthen my faith, transform my mind, and learn to see and love myself the way God sees and loves me.

At the end of writing this devotional, God gave me a vision. I saw myself dressed in armor, not only representing myself, but a multitude of women. This armor symbolized everything I needed to endure the process of transformation. By the end, this armor—strong and shining—was as if it were brand new, just like my spirit. I wanted to conclude this devotional with the Scripture that encapsulates the significance of this armor— a reminder of the strength and renewal we gain through God's guidance.

* * *

Ephesians 6:10-20 (AMP)

[10] *In conclusion, be strong in the Lord [draw your strength from Him and be empowered through your union with Him] and in the power of His [boundless] might.*

[11] *Put on the full armor of God [for His precepts are like the splendid armor of a heavily-armed soldier], so that you may be able to [successfully] stand up against all the schemes and the strategies and the deceits of the devil.*

[12] *For our struggle is not against flesh and blood [contending only with physical opponents], but against the rulers, against the powers, against the world forces of this [present] darkness, against the spiritual forces of wickedness in the heavenly (supernatural) places.*

[13] *Therefore, put on the complete armor of God, so that you will be able to [successfully] resist and stand your ground in the evil day [of danger], and having done everything [that the crisis demands], to stand firm [in your place, fully prepared, immovable, victorious].*

[14] *So stand firm and hold your ground, having tightened the wide band of truth (personal integrity, moral courage) around your waist and having put on the breastplate of righteousness (an upright heart),*

[15] *and having strapped on your feet the gospel of peace in preparation [to face the enemy with firm-footed stability and the readiness produced by the good news].*

¹⁶ Above all, lift up the [protective] shield of faith with which you can extinguish all the flaming arrows of the evil one.

¹⁷ And take the helmet of salvation, and the sword of the Spirit, which is the Word of God.

¹⁸ With all prayer and petition pray [with specific requests] at all times [on every occasion and in every season] in the Spirit, and with this in view, stay alert with all perseverance and petition [interceding in prayer] for all God's people.

¹⁹ And pray *for me, that words may be given to me when I open my mouth, to proclaim boldly the mystery of the good news [of salvation],*

²⁰ for which I am an ambassador in chains. And pray *that in* proclaiming *it I may speak boldly* and *courageously, as I should.*

ACKNOWLEDGMENTS

I want to give a very special and heartwarming thank you to the love of my life, *Dashawn Wingate*, whose words just three months into dating were, "I'm in love with the person you're becoming." Mind you, at that time, I didn't even know who that would be.

* * *

DaShawn— you saw me before I saw myself. You valued me before I knew I was someone to be valued. You encouraged me through every valley I walked. You stayed with me through my suicide attempts and hospitalizations. You loved me when I felt I didn't deserve to be loved. You have taken "in sickness and in health" to a whole other level.

I am so grateful God has blessed me with someone I can trust with my life and the lives of my children. Thank you for your patience in allowing me to heal and discover who I am, never rushing the process. You are a rare gem, and I am excited to continue this beautiful life we have created, which God has so richly blessed us with. *I love you, babe!*

About the Author

Candice is first a wife and mother to three beautiful children. She has spent the last six years studying and training under Prophetess Karen B. Knight's ministry, *A Prophetic Cry Global Alliance*, as a prophetess and psalmist. Currently, she and her husband are pastoring one of Prophetess Karen B. Knight's leg ministries, *Generation Now: Young Adult Bible Study*, where they virtually teach young adults in various states about the love of God and how to live a Holy Spirit-led life, seeking first His kingdom and His righteousness. In addition to this, God has commissioned Candice to help women know His love and break free from the bondage of low self-esteem and depression, as part of her ministerial assignment through her business, Uplifting Beauty LLC. She is just scratching the surface of what God has in store for her life.

* * *

To get in touch with Candice A. Wingate, please contact her here:

Email: upliftingbeautyllc@outlook.com
Website: www.upliftingbeautyllc.store

www.ingramcontent.com/pod-product-compliance
Lightning Source LLC
Chambersburg PA
CBHW051545120626
46551CB00013B/1368